dinosaurs

This edition published by Fog City Press
Conceived and produced by Weldon Owen Pty Ltd
61 Victoria Street, McMahons Point
Sydney, NSW 2060, Australia

Group Chief Executive Officer John Owen
President and Chief Executive Officer Terry Newell
Publisher Sheena Coupe
Creative Director Sue Burk
Vice President, International Sales Stuart Laurence
Vice President, Sales and New Business Development Amy Kaneko
Vice President, Sales: Asia and Latin America Dawn Low
Administrator, International Sales Kristine Ravn
Publishing Coordinator Mike Crowton

Consultant Editor Denise Ryan
Managing Editor Jessica Cox
Editor Helen Flint
Designer Gabrielle Green

ISBN: 978-1-74089-664-1

Color reproduction by SC (Sang Choy) International Pte Ltd
Printed by SNP Leefung Printers Ltd
Manufactured in China

10 9 8 7 6 5 4 3 2 1

A WELDON OWEN PRODUCTION

my first

encyclopedia of

dinosaurs

Denise Ryan

FOG CITY PRESS

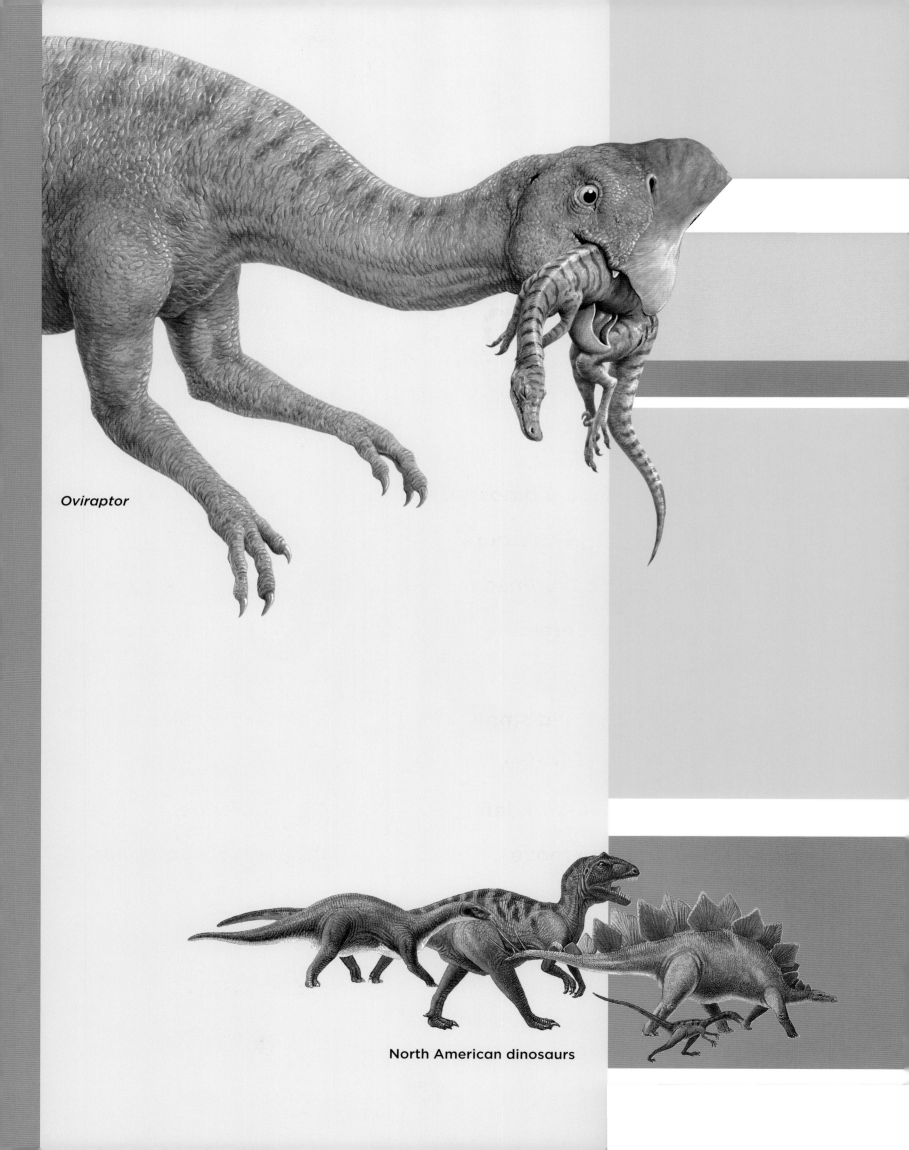

Oviraptor

North American dinosaurs

contents

Deinonychus

6 What is a dinosaur?

8 Age of dinosaurs

10 Inside a dinosaur

12 Meat eaters

14 Plant eaters

16 Large and small

18 Fast and slow

20 Attack and defense

22 On the move

24 Dinosaur babies

26 Sharing their world

28 Disappearing act

30 Great hunters

32 *Archaeopteryx*

34 *Tyrannosaurus*

36 *Deinonychus*

38 *Diplodocus*

40 *Parasaurolophus*

42 *Stegosaurus*

44 *Triceratops*

46 Glossary

48 Index

What is a dinosaur?

Dinosaurs were very special reptiles that lived on Earth for about 160 million years. Some dinosaurs were as small as chickens but others were huge. They had scaly skin and their eggs had shells. Dinosaurs walked upright and stood on either four legs or two.

Brachiosaurus

Deinonychus

Hypsilophodon

Ouranosaurus

Tyrannosaurus

Dinosaur parade

There were at least 1,000 different types of dinosaurs. There were dinosaurs with horns and crests and others with spikes and razor-sharp claws.

Parasaurolophus

Struthiomimus

Triceratops

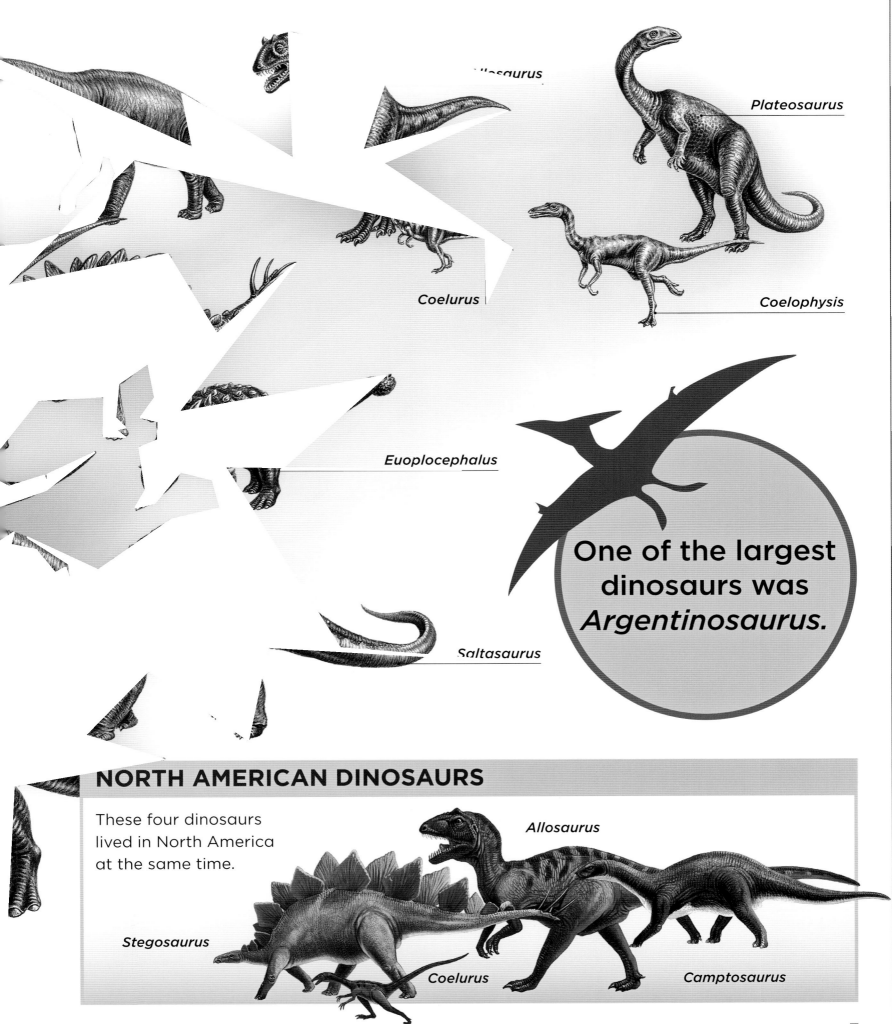

Plateosaurus

Coelurus

Coelophysis

Euoplocephalus

Saltasaurus

One of the largest dinosaurs was *Argentinosaurus.*

NORTH AMERICAN DINOSAURS

These four dinosaurs lived in North America at the same time.

Allosaurus

Stegosaurus

Coelurus

Camptosaurus

Age of dinosaurs

Dinosaurs first appeared on Earth about 228 million years ago. Millions of years later, as Earth's landmasses drifted apart, the weather changed. The cooler, wet weather was perfect for dinosaurs, so many more developed. About 65 million years ago, these extraordinary creatures disappeared.

Catching food
Dilophosaurus could run after its prey on its strong back legs.

Tyrannosaurus

Pteranodon

Dinosaur times

The time that dinosaurs roamed Earth is divided into three periods—the Triassic, Jurassic, and Cretaceous. The dinosaurs on these pages come from the three different periods.

Diplodocus

Dinosaurs lived millions of years before our first human ancestors.

Inside a dinosaur

All dinosaurs had skeletons inside their bodies. These gave them strength and protected their soft organs. Dinosaurs also had large muscles that helped them move around. The skeletons, muscles, and organs were all covered with a layer of thick, scaly skin.

Long journey

Apatosaurus ate a huge amount of leaves. The leaves traveled from its mouth to its stomach, along a long tube.

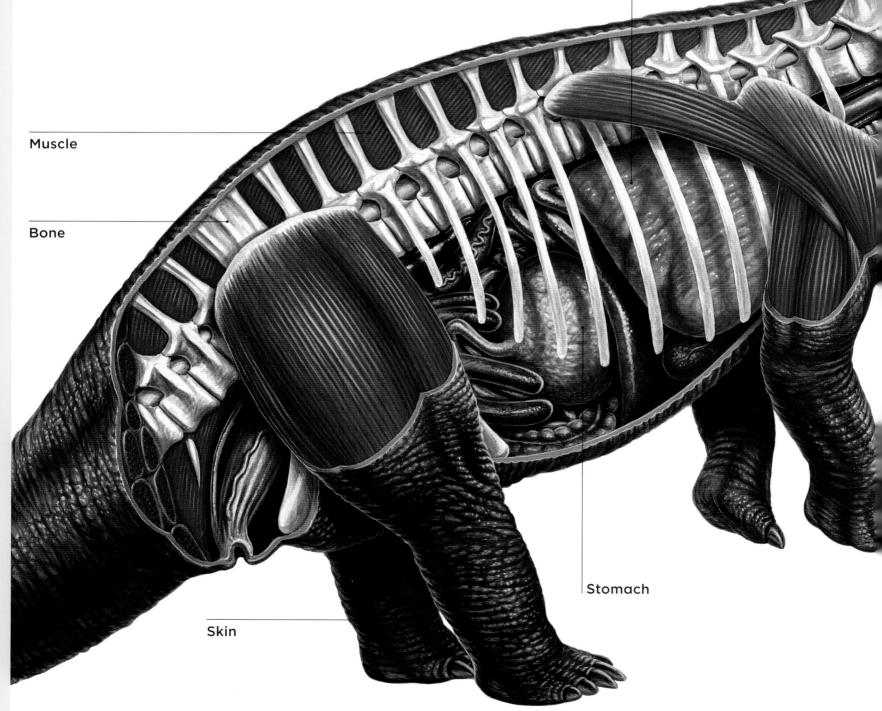

Lung

Muscle

Bone

Stomach

Skin

Long neck

Fossil

Fossils have helped us know a lot about dinosaurs. Fossils are the remains of dinosaurs that have turned to stone.

A *Tyrannosaurus* heart was probably as big as a person.

Skeleton

Some dinosaurs' bones were filled with tiny holes, which helped them stay very light.

Meat eaters

Some meat-eating dinosaurs ate prey larger than themselves. Others ate smaller food, such as eggs and insects. Meat-eating dinosaurs all had short, muscular bodies with low, powerful tails, and strong back legs.

WHAT IS FOR LUNCH

A dinosaur's lunch often included lizards, small mammals, eggs, fish, and insects.

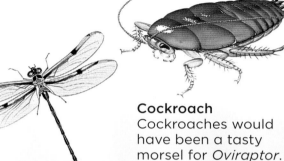

Cockroach
Cockroaches would have been a tasty morsel for *Oviraptor*.

Dragonfly
Gallimimus would have snapped up dragonflies.

Lunchtime
Dinosaurs used their hands, teeth, or sharp beaks to catch and eat their food.

Hand it to me
Compsognathus liked lizard lunches.

Ferocious foe
Deinonychus had long, slashing claws on its back legs, which it used to attack prey.

Deinonychus

Hooked
Baryonyx enjoyed fish for lunch.

One gulp
Gallimimus snapped up small animals.

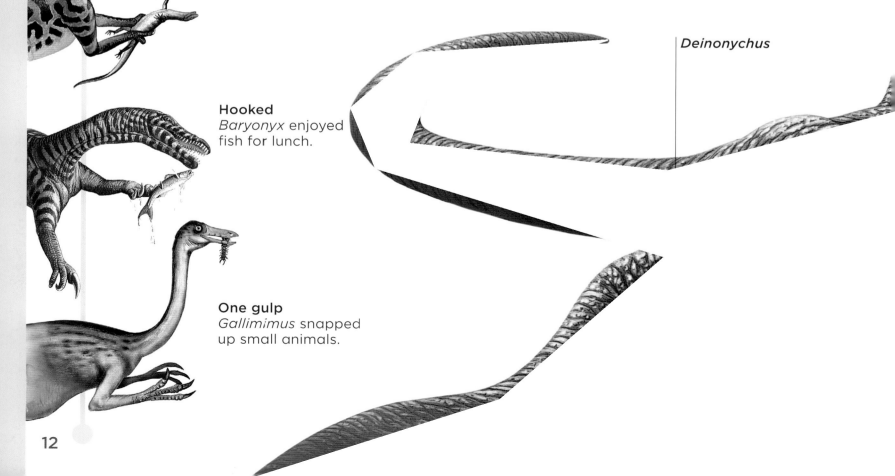

Tenontosaurus

Spinosaurus was the largest meat-eating dinosaur.

Plant eaters

Plant-eating dinosaurs ate ferns, treetops, pinecones, and flowering plants. Many of them had special cheeks in which they stored the plants while they were chewing. Some had different kinds of teeth for cutting and grinding.

Plant eaters

Plant-eating dinosaurs came in many shapes and sizes.

There were hundreds of different plant-eating dinosaurs.

Heterodontosaurus
This dinosaur may have used its hands to pick up the plants it ate.

Eat up

The plant-eating sauropods were the biggest dinosaurs of all. They had to eat huge quantities of plants to provide them with enough energy to live.

Centrosaurus
The strong jaws of *Centrosaurus* sheared through stems and leaves.

TREE MEALS

Plant-eating dinosaurs often ate tough leaves from cycads, trees, and ferns.

Ginkgo
The ginkgo tree is one of the plants that dinosaurs ate.

Horsetail
Horsetails grew into large trees, which the dinosaurs ate, too.

Stomach stones
Sauropods could not break up their food with their teeth so they swallowed stones. These ground up the plants in their stomachs.

Large tail
The sauropods had large tails to help them balance.

Large and small

Dinosaurs were the biggest, heaviest, and longest land animals that have ever lived. However, there were actually more small dinosaurs than large ones. Here is how some of the biggest and smallest measure up.

Size matters

Three of the biggest dinosaurs that we know of were found in the United States. They were *Supersaurus*, *Giraffatitan,* and *Seismosaurus.*

Heaviest

The heaviest dinosaur is *Brachiosaurus,* which was as tall as a four-story building.

Longest

Diplodocus is the longest known dinosaur. It used its tail to defend itself against its foes.

Smallest

One of the smallest known dinosaurs is *Compsognathus.*

The longest dinosaur name is *Micropachy-cephalosaurus.*

Biggest?
For many years, *Tyrannosaurus* was known as the largest ever meat eater. Now we know of other, larger ones.

Fast and slow

Fast-moving dinosaurs usually had small, streamlined bodies and long back legs. They could run quickly to escape their larger, more powerful enemies. The big, plant-eating dinosaurs slowly lumbered along, shaking the ground around them as they walked.

The fastest dinosaur would leave the fastest human far behind.

Slow down
Diplodocus and *Apatosaurus* were slow-moving beasts with large bodies and long necks and tails.

Diplodocus

Apatosaurus

You cannot catch me!

Gallimimus could race along at speeds of up to 30 miles per hour (48 km/h). It could change direction suddenly too, so it could easily dodge out of the reach of *Albertosaurus*.

Albertosaurus

Gallimimus

Big and slow

Tyrannosaurus was so big and heavy that it could run only as fast as the fastest human.

Attack and defense

Dinosaurs had to fight for their survival. They needed to find enough to eat while making sure they were not eaten themselves. Meat eaters used their claws or teeth to attack their prey. Plant eaters had horns, spikes, armor, or tail clubs for protection.

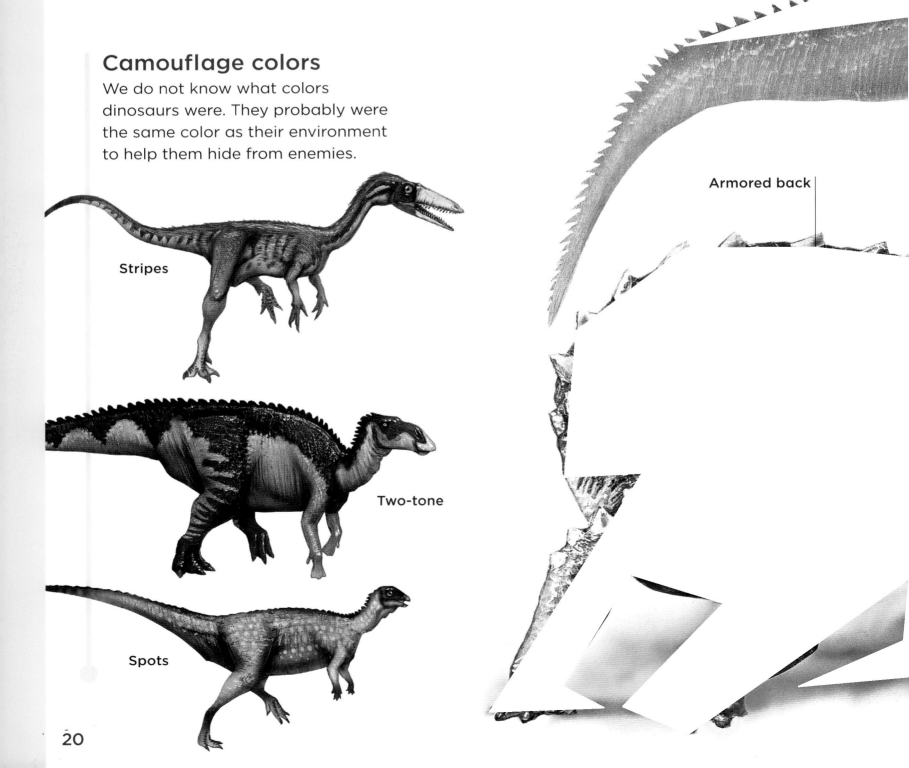

Camouflage colors

We do not know what colors dinosaurs were. They probably were the same color as their environment to help them hide from enemies.

Stripes

Two-tone

Spots

Armored back

On the attack

Ankylosaurus used its tail to attack. However, one bite from the powerful *Tyrannosaurus* could finish it off.

Tail club

Sharp teeth

DEFENSE WEAPONS

Euoplocephalus tail

Euoplocephalus protected itself with a bony club at the end of its tail. *Tuojiangosaurus* defended itself with its stabbing, spiked tail.

Tuojiangosaurus tail

On the move

Plant-eating dinosaurs often moved in herds to search for fresh food. Some herds had more than 10,000 dinosaurs in them. Meat eaters, such as *Tyrannosaurus*, lurked behind the thundering group, ready to attack any weak or sick animals.

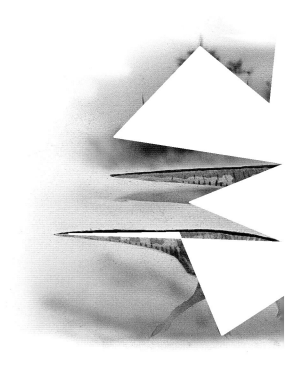

Solitary
Because it lived alone, *Euoplocephalus* defended itself with its bony armor and a club on its tail.

Race against time
A herd of crested *Corythosaurus* and horned *Chasmosaurus* race across a North American plain in search of food.

How do we know?
When dinosaurs walked through mud, they left footprints. Fossils of these footprints show that many dinosaurs traveled in groups.

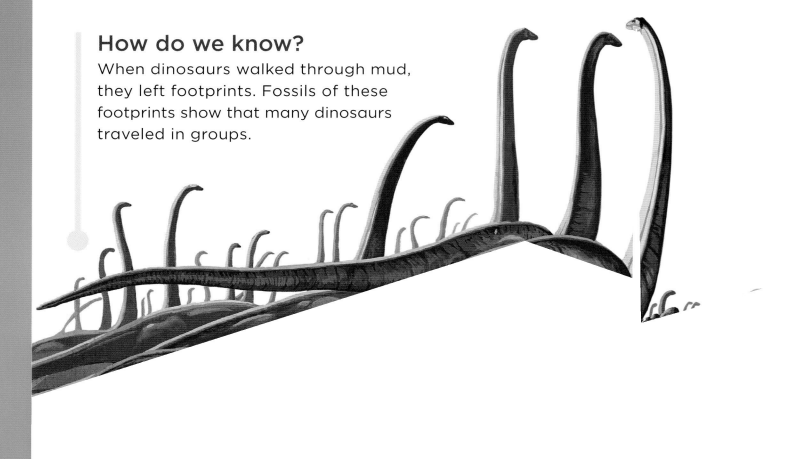

Moving in large herds was safer than traveling alone.

Dinosaur babies

Dinosaurs laid eggs, built nests, and cared for their young as they hatched. They fed their babies until they were ready to leave the nest. Each dinosaur had its own way of doing things. Most acted more like birds than reptiles when they looked after their young.

The biggest dinosaur egg that has been found is as big as a football!

Dinosaur nursery
Maiasaura nests, scooped out of the mud, contained up to twenty-five hatchlings.

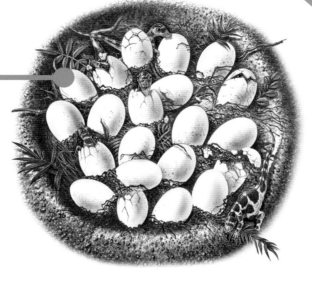

Baby
Oviraptor

GROWING UP

Here is a one-year-old *Maiasaura* and an adult *Maiasaura*. What differences can you see?

Adult

One year old

Mother
Oviraptor

Feeding time

A mother *Oviraptor* has freshly killed prey for her hungry babies.

Sharing their world

While dinosaurs ruled the land, flying reptiles soared through the sky. Long-necked plesiosaurs and dolphin-like ichthyosaurs raced through the seas searching for fish. Turtles and crocodiles swam in the oceans, and early mammals started to appear.

Magnolia

The magnolia is an ancient flowering plant. Plant-eating dinosaurs probably ate them.

NEIGHBORS

Many different creatures lived alongside the ruling dinosaurs.

Kannemeyeria
This plant eater lived on land.

Ichthyosaurus
The dolphin-like *Ichthyosaurus* could swim at high speeds.

Swimming
Cryptoclidus swims after a school of fish.

Similar

Some creatures that lived in the time of the dinosaurs look similar to animals that are alive today.

Mammals
Mammals such as this little *Alphadon* lived in the age of the dinosaurs.

Snakes and lizards
Pachyrhachis was one of the earliest known snakes.

Moths and bees
Tiny moths and bees first appeared during the time of the dinosaurs.

Sea and sky

Scaphognathus flies through the air, swooping to catch a meal of fish, while *Cryptoclidus* swims through the water.

Flying
Scaphognathus swoops out of the sky.

Disappearing act

Nobody knows why the dinosaurs disappeared. Some think that a huge meteorite hit Earth, causing dust clouds, acid rain, storms, and huge waves. Others think that many volcanoes erupted and caused the climate to change.

Why did they disappear?

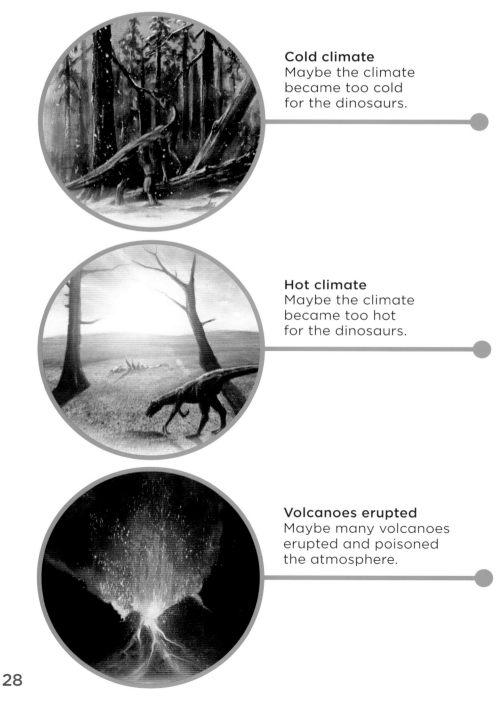

Cold climate
Maybe the climate became too cold for the dinosaurs.

Hot climate
Maybe the climate became too hot for the dinosaurs.

Volcanoes erupted
Maybe many volcanoes erupted and poisoned the atmosphere.

The end of an era

When the dinosaurs vanished, some small mammals and reptiles survived. Turtles and crocodiles are still alive today, but the dinosaurs are gone forever.

All gone
All the large land animals died out.

Mammals
Small mammals survived the time of the dinosaurs.

Great hunters

People who hunt for dinosaur fossils are called paleontologists. They know where to look, and often spend hours searching in places where fossils have been found before. Paleontologists use picks, shovels, trowels, and brushes to uncover the fossils.

Digging carefully

These paleontologists are working on a dig site. Some of them are uncovering the remains of a hadrosaur, while others are making a map of the skeleton.

DOWN IN THE SWAMP

Dozens of dinosaurs died in swamps. The swamps gradually became coal beds and the dinosaur skeletons became fossils. Millions of years later, some of these fossils have been found.

Hide and seek

Fossils can be found in many different types of rock. There are some places on Earth where the rocks are packed full of dinosaur fossils.

Paleontologists

Jigsaw puzzle

When dinosaur bones have been dug up, copies are made. The copies are stuck together to display in museums.

| Dinosaur fossil

Archaeopteryx

People did not know if *Archaeopteryx* was a bird or a dinosaur when it was first discovered. Now we know it was a bird that lived alongside the dinosaurs. It had large wings that were covered in feathers, big eyes, and a beak that was filled with small teeth.

The name *Archaeopteryx* means "ancient wing."

Fossil

This fossil shows the feathers and skeleton of *Archaeopteryx*. The fossil is about 150 million years old.

Wing

Head

Taii

Flying food

Archaeopteryx was a meat eater. It lived near the sea and probably hunted small fish and insects.

Feathers
Archaeopteryx had large wings covered in feathers.

Wing

Food
Archaeopteryx probably ate insects, such as this dragonfly.

WINGS

Birds that live today are related to *Archaeopteryx*. Their wing bones and feathers are almost the same.

Archaeopteryx wing | Pigeon wing

Tyrannosaurus

Tyrannosaurus had strong jaws for crunching through flesh and bone, and a good sense of smell. *Tyrannosaurus* had big back legs, but could not run very quickly. It probably survived on meat it could find from dinosaurs that were already dead.

Huge teeth

Tyrannosaurus had a mouth filled with teeth. Each tooth had rough edges to help it saw through meat and bone.

BIG JAW

Meat-eating dinosaurs, such as *Tyrannosaurus,* had jaws that could open wide so they could swallow large chunks of flesh.

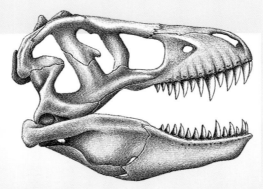

Walking

Tyrannosaurus walked on long back legs. Its front legs were small and had no known use.

Front legs

Tyrannosaurus teeth were as big as bananas!

Open wide

Tyrannosaurus had powerful jaws and large, sharp teeth. If one of its teeth fell out, another would grow to take its place.

Deinonychus

Deinonychus used the three-clawed fingers on its large hands to snatch small prey or wound large animals. *Deinonychus* walked and ran on its outer toes, which had long, sharp claws. Its stiff tail helped *Deinonychus* to change direction suddenly when it was running to catch prey.

The name *Deinonychus* means "terrible claw."

Bony rods
If you look carefully at this skeleton you can see the bony rods of its tail.

PACK HUNTER

Deinonychus lived and hunted in packs, much like today's wolves. Its close relative *Velociraptor* also lived in packs. This pack of *Velociraptors* is attacking a *Bactrosaurus*.

No hope
The *Bactrosaurus* is helpless when attacked by a pack.

Deinonychus may have been able to turn in midair while leaping to catch its prey.

Terrible claw

Deinonychus feet each had three sharply clawed toes. The "terrible claw" was on the second toe of each foot. It could swivel around.

Diplodocus

Diplodocus was a large plant-eating dinosaur with a long tail and neck. It could use its tail like a whip to lash at attackers. The head and brain of *Diplodocus* were tiny compared to its body, but its eyes were large and its teeth were long and thin.

Whip tail

Diplodocus could use its tail to whip at its enemies.

WADING THROUGH WATER

Diplodocus could move through shallow water by floating its heavy body on the surface and moving forward with its front feet.

How long?

Diplodocus was as long as 20 children lying end-to-end!

Long neck

Standing tall

Diplodocus could stand up on its back legs to scare away enemies. This also helped it reach leaves on tall trees.

A *Diplodocus* head was the same size as a horse's head.

Parasaurolophus

Parasaurolophus had a large, hollow crest on the top of its head. It used this crest to make loud noises. *Parasaurolophus* had a beak, rather like a duck's, and a mouth filled with small teeth. It used these to rip up and chew plants.

Hot air
Parasaurolophus blew air from its mouth into its crest, then out its nose. This created a loud sound.

Meal time
Parasaurolophus leant forward on its short front legs to eat.

Different shapes
Male and female *Parasaurolophus* had different-shaped heads.

Male

Female

Group life

Parasaurolophus lived in herds. It could "talk" to the other members of its group using loud sounds it made with its head.

The crest of *Parasaurolophus* could grow as long as a fully grown man is tall.

Strange heads

Parasaurolophus was not the only dinosaur with a strangely shaped head!

Stegoceras

Lambeosaurus

Stegosaurus

Stegosaurus was a huge dinosaur with heavily built back legs and short front legs. It had flat plates along its backbone, from its neck down to the middle of its tail. *Stegosaurus* had a short head with a long snout and small teeth.

Leg work

The short front legs of *Stegosaurus* helped it to keep its head low, close to the short plants that it ate.

Stegosaurus spikes may have acted like a built-in air conditioner.

Tail

Colorful creatures

Stegosaurus may have been colored to blend in with the plants it lived near.

Head down
Stegosaurus kept its head down close to food.

Plant eaters
Stegosaurus ate ferns and other plants.

RELATIVES

Tuojiangosaurus and *Kentrosaurus* are thought to be close relatives of *Stegosaurus.* Can you see how similar they are?

Tuojiangosaurus

Kentrosaurus

Triceratops

Triceratops was a plant-eating dinosaur that traveled around in small groups. Its large, strong body and horned head were similar to that of a rhinoceros. It moved slowly, but it could use its armor of horns and a bony neck frill to fight off attackers.

Horn

Charge!

When an enemy attacked, *Triceratops* would charge. Its sharp horns would scare away most attackers.

Head case

Some dinosaurs had head plates. *Chasmosaurus* used its head plate to help it find a mate. *Centrosaurus* used its head plate to fight enemies.

Chasmosaurus

Centrosaurus

ONE OF THE LAST

Triceratops was roaming Earth toward the end of the age of dinosaurs. It was probably one of the last of the dinosaurs.

Bony neck frill

The name *Triceratops* means "three-horned face."

Legs
Triceratops had thick, strong legs.

Glossary

Tyrannosaurus

Euoplocephalus

acid rain
Rain that has harmful gases in it

ancestors
Early peoples to whom we are related

ancient
Existed in times long, long ago

armor
A covering that keeps something safe

atmosphere
A mixture of gases that surrounds Earth

climate
The weather conditions of a place during a full year

crests
Growths at the top of animals' heads

cycads
An ancient group of seed plants

environment
The surrounding conditions

erupted
Forced out violently

fleet-footed
Able to move swiftly

foes
Enemies or opponents

hadrosaur
A duck-billed dinosaur

hatchlings
Baby dinosaurs

herds
Groups of animals that live together

ichthyosaurs
Giant sea reptiles

mammals
Animals whose young feed on their mothers' milk

Dilophosaurus

Scaphognathus

meteorite
A small, solid body from space that reaches Earth's surface

muscles
Tissues made up of fibers that help bodies move

paleontologist
A scientist who studies fossils

plesiosaurs
Flippered sea reptiles with long necks

predators
Animals that live by hunting and feeding on other animals

prey
Any animal hunted or killed by another animal

reptiles
Cold-blooded, air-breathing animals

sauropods
Large, four-legged, plant-eating dinosaurs with long necks and small heads

theropods
Meat-eating dinosaurs that walked on two legs and had clawed feet

volcanoes
Breaks in Earth's crust through which gases and lava escape

Index

A

acid rain 28
Albertosaurus 19
Allosaurus 7
Alphadon 27, 29
Ankylosaurus 21
Apatosaurus 10, 18
Archaeopteryx 32–3
armor 20, 22, 44
attack 20–1, 45

B

babies 24–5
Bactrosaurus 36
Baryonyx 12
birds 32
bones 10–11, 30–1
Brachiosaurus 6, 16

C

camouflage 20, 42
Centrosaurus 14, 44
Chasmosaurus 14, 44
claws 20, 21, 36–7
climate change 28
cockroach 12
Coelophysis 7
Coelurus 7
color 20, 42
Compsognathus 12, 16
Corythosaurus 22
crest 40
Cretaceous Period 9
Cryptoclidus 24

D

defense 20–1, 22
Deinonychus 6, 12, 36–7
digging up dinosaurs 30–1
Dilophosaurus 8
Diplodocus 9, 16, 18, 38–9
dust clouds 28
Dystylosaurus 14

E

eggs 24–5
Euoplocephalus 7, 21, 22
extinction 8, 28–9

F

fast dinosaurs 18–19
feathers 32
food 8, 10, 12–15, 22, 32, 34, 36, 39, 40
footprints 22
fossils 11, 14, 22, 30–1, 32

G

Gallimimus 12, 19
ginkgo 15

H

heaviest dinosaur 16
herds 22, 44
Heterodontosaurus 14
horns 20, 45
horsetails 15
hunting 8, 34, 36
Hypsilophodon 6

I

ichthyosaurs 26
Ichthyosaurus 26
insects 12, 27, 32

J

jaws 34–5
Jurassic Period 9

K

Kannemeyeria 26
Kentrosaurus 43

L

Lambeosaurus 41
legs 6, 12, 18, 34, 42
lizards 12, 27
longest dinosaur 16

M

magnolia 26
Maiasaura 24
mammals 26
meat-eating dinosaurs 12–13, 20, 22, 32, 34, 36
meteorite 28
Micropachycephalosaurus 17
migration 22–3
muscles 10

N

nests 24

O

Ouranosaurus 6
Oviraptor 24–5

P

Pachyrhachis 27
paleontologists 30–1
Parasaurolophus 6, 40–1
plant-eating dinosaurs 9, 13, 14–15, 20, 22, 38, 40, 42, 44
plants 15, 26
Plateosaurus 7
plesiosaurs 26
Pteranodon 7

R

reproduction 24–5
reptiles 12, 29

S

Saltasaurus 7
sauropods 9, 14
Scaphognathus 27
sea crocodiles 26
sea dragons 26
size 6, 11, 16–17, 26, 38
skeleton 10–11, 30–1, 36
skin 6, 10
slow dinosaurs 18–19, 34
smallest dinosaur 16
sound 40
speed 18–19, 34
spikes 20
spots 20
Stegoceras 41
Stegosaurus 7, 42–3
stomach stones 15
stripes 20
Struthiomimus 6
Supersaurus 16
swimming 26–7, 38

T

tails 15, 18, 20–1, 22, 36, 38, 42
teeth 20, 33, 34–5, 38, 40, 42
Tenontosaurus 13
Triassic Period 9
Triceratops 6, 44–5
Tuojiangosaurus 21, 43
turtles 26, 29
Tyrannosaurus 6, 7, 8, 11, 13, 17, 19, 22, 34–5

V

Velociraptor 25, 36
volcanic eruptions 28

W

weather changes 8, 28
wings 33

Credits